To the Reader...

Our purpose in creating this series is to provide young readers with accurate accounts of the lives of Native American men and women important in the history of their tribes. The stories are written by scholars, including American Indians.

Native Americans are as much a part of North American life today as they were one hundred years ago. Even in times past, Indians were not all the same. Not all of them lived in teepees or wore feather warbonnets. They were not all warriors. Some did fight against the white man, but many befriended him.

Whether patriot or politician, athlete or artist, Arapaho or Zuni, the story of each person in this series deserves to be told. Whether the individuals gained distinction on the battlefield or the playing field, in the courtroom or the classroom, they have enriched the heritage and history of all Americans. It is hoped that those who read their stories will realize that many different peoples, regardless of culture or color, have played a part in shaping the United States and Canada, in making both countries what they are today.

Herman J. Viola
General Editor
Author of *Exploring the West*
and other volumes on the West
and Native Americans

GENERAL EDITOR
Herman J. Viola
Author of *Exploring the West* and other volumes on the West
and American Indians

MANAGING EDITOR
Robert M. Kvasnicka
Coeditor of *The Commissioners of Indian Affairs, 1824–1977*
Coeditor of *Indian-White Relations: A Persistent Paradox*

MANUSCRIPT EDITOR
Barbara J. Behm

DESIGNER
Kathleen A. Hartnett

PRODUCTION
Andrew Rupniewski

Eileen Rickey

First Steck-Vaughn Edition 1993

Library of Congress Number: 89-10430

3 4 5 6 7 8 9   95 94 93 92

Library of Congress Cataloging-in-Publication Data

Doss, Michael P.
    Plenty Coups.
    (Raintree American Indian stories)
    Summary: Examines the life of the famed warrior and Crow
Indian chief, who performed eighty feats of valor in combat during
his youth but never warred against the United States.
    1. Plenty Coups, Chief of the Crows, 1848-1932—Juvenile
literature.   2. Crow Indians—Biography—Juvenile literature.
3. Indians of North America—Great Plains—Biography—Juvenile
literature.   [1. Plenty Coups, Chief of the Crows, 1848-1932.
2. Crow Indians—Biography.   3. Indians of North America—
Great Plains—Biography] I. Title. II. Series.
E99.C92P553   1989   978′.004975 [B]   [92]   89-10430
ISBN 0-8172-3409-8   hardcover library binding
ISBN 0-8114-4089-3   softcover binding

PLENTY COUPS

Text by Michael P. Doss
Illustrations by Yoshi Miyake

A RIVILO BOOK

RSVP
RAINTREE
STECK-VAUGHN
PUBLISHERS
The Steck-Vaughn Company

Chief Plenty Coups (pronounced "cooz") was the last
traditional chief of the Crow Nation. When he died in 1932,
the Crow Nation honored him by saying that it would have
no more chiefs because no one would ever be able to match
the achievements of Plenty Coups. Every leader of the Crow
Nation since the time of Plenty Coups has been called
chairman rather than chief.

Ten years earlier, Plenty Coups had been honored by
other American Indian tribes. Chiefs from many tribes all
over the United States had selected him "Chief of Chiefs."
He would represent all the tribes at the dedication of the
Tomb of the Unknown Soldier at Arlington National
Cemetery in Virginia.

On November 11, 1921, President Warren G. Harding, his wife, and many foreign and United States government officials heard the chief give a short speech. Many people considered the speech a masterpiece. As he placed his warbonnet, coup stick, and the flag of the Crow Nation on the Tomb of the Unknown Soldier, Plenty Coups said in the Crow language, "I am told that this soldier is one who is known only to God. If that is the case, this soldier, known only to 'The Maker,' could well be an American Indian. With all of the honors being extended to him this day, by all of the countries that were in the war, he truly is a chief. And, in keeping with the rites that we extend to a departed chief, I hereby dedicate this grave as the gravesite of a chief." Plenty Coups's beautiful eagle feather bonnet, coup stick, and flag are displayed in the Trophy Room at Arlington National Cemetery.

During the dedication activities, Plenty Coups met Ferdinand Foch. He was a marshal of the French army who had served as commander of all the Allied forces in World War I. Marshal Foch liked the chief so much that when he made his triumphal tour of the United States, he had his train routed from Billings, Montana, to the Crow Agency so that he could visit Plenty Coups.

The Crow call themselves the Apsaroka People. *Apsaroka* means "children of the large-beaked bird," or "raven." They are actually the Raven People. Non-Indians incorrectly called them the Crow, and that is the name by which they are known.

Plenty Coups was born in 1848 at a place known to the Crow People as "The-Cliff-That-Has-No-Pass." It is near what is now the city of Billings, Montana, on the Yellowstone River, known by the Crows to this very day as Elk River. His mother was called Otter-Woman. His father was Medicine Bird.

When he was an old man, Plenty Coups talked about his life to Frank B. Linderman, a writer. He told Linderman about his childhood. He told him how Crow children learned at an early age to run long distances, to swim, and to use a bow and arrow. To learn endurance, his grandfather had him chase butterflies. When he caught one, his grandfather told him, "Rub its wings over your heart, my son, and ask the butterflies to lend you their grace and swiftness."

The Crow, like other Plains Indians, relied upon buffalo, bighorn sheep, elk, deer, roots, berries, and fruits for their food. In order to get large amounts of buffalo meat, herds of buffalo were sometimes stampeded over a cliff to their deaths. The Crow were careful that none of the meat, hides, or bones of the buffalo was wasted. What wasn't used for food was used for making clothing and tools. Plenty Coups recalled that buffalo were "not only our food but our clothing and shelter. The other animals furnished only a change of meat and summer clothes. The buffalo was everything to us."

Although Plenty Coups had a dream that told him the buffalo would vanish, most Indians thought the buffalo would always be on the earth. Lightning Woman, an elderly Crow woman, remembered that when she was a child, her people once had to wait twenty-four hours for a huge herd of buffalo to stampede across their path. But, due to the trade in buffalo hides by non-Indians, the buffalo had disappeared by 1884. When that happened, Plenty Coups said, the Crow "became a changed people."

The name *Plenty Coups* meant "Many Achievements." Plenty Coups received his name from his grandfather. His grandfather had dreamed that the boy would count many coups—or perform many brave deeds—and would live to be an old man and an honored chief. Because of his name, Plenty Coups said he felt "obliged to excel my companions, to be a leader among those of my own age." He earned his first coup (or honor) when he was nine years old by an act that required exceptional courage. He confronted a wounded and dangerous bull buffalo. Using only his bow, he struck the animal twice at the root of the tail. Plenty Coups then managed to get away before the angry animal could trample him.

On countless occasions, Plenty Coups took part in or led raiding parties against the many enemy tribes that surrounded "Crow Country." Horses were highly prized by the Crow, who were among the finest horsemen in all the world. Since horses represented wealth, they were one of the favorite targets of Crow raiders. It was considered an honor to take horses from an enemy camp without being caught. A warrior could count a special coup for capturing a horse tied to a lodge in an enemy camp.

Plenty Coups performed over eighty brave deeds in combat. He was soon recognized as the "War Chief of the Crow Nation," a title he would carry all his life. The Crow's enemies were among the most powerful tribes in North America. They were the Sioux, Shoshone, Arapaho, Piegan, Blood, Blackfeet, Cheyenne, Flathead, Assiniboin, and Gros Ventre tribes. The Crow always had to fight to survive, since they were a small tribe. Plenty Coups remembered that when he was still a child he "realized the constant danger my people were in from enemies on every side. Our country is the most beautiful of all. Its rivers and plains, its mountains and timberlands, where there was always plenty of meat and berries, attracted other tribes. And they wished to possess it for their own."

As a means of protecting their country, the Crow decided to share it. They invited other tribes to come to Crow Country to hunt and gather berries and plums. But they warned them not to stay too long. If they did, they would be attacked and pushed out. In order to protect their beautiful Crow Country, the greatly outnumbered Crow had to be better warriors than their enemies. And they were. No better proof of this is needed than to know that the Crow were able to keep their lands.

During his life, Chief Plenty Coups had many visions or dreams. In order to receive a vision, an Indian had to go without food and water for at least four days and nights. This was usually done on a mountaintop. Plenty Coups received his most important vision after he cut off the end of the first finger of his left hand. It was from this dream that he saw the coming of the white man in numbers too great to fight and win. Also during this dream, he saw the passing of the buffalo and the coming of the "spotted buffalo," or cattle.

It was during this dream that the young Plenty Coups received his protective "medicine." Indian "medicine" often took the form of animals, who told the vision seekers in dreams that they are their protectors. Most Indians carried "medicine bundles" that held things connected with their medicine. Plenty Coups's medicine was the little bird known as the chickadee. Though small, the chickadee is an excellent listener. It is the least in physical strength but the strongest in mind among its kind. Plenty Coups was told in his dream, "Develop your body, but do not neglect your mind, Plenty Coups. It is the mind that leads a man to power, not strength of body."

Since Plenty Coups knew from his vision that his Crow people must learn to live peacefully with the whites, he looked for a way to have a friendly relationship with them. He knew that this was the only hope of keeping his sacred Crow Country for future generations of his people. An opportunity came in 1876 when the United States Army asked the Crow for help against the Sioux, Cheyenne, and Arapaho. Plenty Coups told the Crow to help the army. In those days, the enemies of the whites were already the enemies of the Crow. When the war was over, the army would remember that the Crow had helped.

Plenty Coups, then twenty-nine years old, took his men and joined General George Crook. The Crow called Crook "Three-Stars." A few Crow warriors were assigned as scouts to serve with Lieutenant Colonel George Custer. The Crow called him "Son of the Morning Star." Custer had ridden into Crow Country at the head of the Seventh Cavalry in June 1876, in order to find the Sioux leader Sitting Bull and his followers.

On June 17, Crook's forces fought the Sioux and
Cheyenne at Rosebud Creek. The Crow, under Plenty
Coups, fought bravely, but they and Crook's men were
defeated. One week later, Custer and 212 of his men were
killed at the Little Bighorn River. The Crow scouts survived
because Custer dismissed them after they warned him not to
attack Sitting Bull and his people. Although the army had
lost their fight against the hostile tribes, the Crow had
proven their friendship to the whites. The Crow Tribe was
the one tribe of the Plains that never made war against the
white man.

As chief of the Crow, Plenty Coups faced many problems that made him call upon the Great Spirit. One of his last challenges came in 1917. By this time, the Crow had been living on a reservation for many years. Thomas J. Walsh, a United States senator from Montana, was trying to pass a bill that would open the Crow Reservation to white people.

Plenty Coups and several subchiefs went to Washington, D.C., to state their feelings against the bill. They were assisted by Robert Yellowtail, a twenty-year-old Crow law student and interpreter.

At sunrise on the day of the final Senate hearings, the chiefs held a medicine-making ceremony with a sacred and powerful medicine bundle at hand. Each chief prayed to the Great Spirit for guidance through this troubling time.

Their prayers were answered. Appearing before a Senate subcommittee, Yellowtail spoke movingly to the senators against opening the Crow Reservation for further settlement. His speech was stopped when the full Senate was called upon to declare war against Germany. After entry into World War I was declared, the senators returned to hear Yellowtail's closing statement. The senators then voted in favor of the Crow Nation. Plenty Coups's "wisdom of the chickadee" had won the day!

Once the United States entered the war, Plenty Coups urged his young Crow men to join the armed forces. He told them that it was a way for them to gain experience as warriors as well as to serve their country.

26

Although Plenty Coups was married several times, he never became a father. He said, "I have no sons or daughters of my own blood, but instead . . . all the Crows are my children, and I love them as a father." He tried to teach his "children" by showing them how to live in a new and strange world changed by newcomers. For example, Plenty Coups made friends with the white people who lived near the reservation. He often invited them to Crow festivals.

He also constructed the first two-story log house in Crow Country. The house at Pryor, Montana, on Sacred Arrow Creek, was one type of home that would take the place of the tepee. His home was sparsely furnished, but one room was entirely devoted to his keepsakes. There he stored his fine clothing, photographs, some weapons, and letters from prominent people. He also built the first dry goods store in the area right next to his home.

In 1928, four years before his death on March 3, 1932, Plenty Coups dedicated his home and land for a "Nations Park" to honor the long and friendly relationship between the Crow Nation and non-Indians. He got the idea for the park when he visited Mount Vernon, the Virginia home of George Washington. He said, "When I walk the slippery log, I want my home to be as the first white chief's. I am the first chief of all Indians, and this will be a tribute to all people from my people—a resting place for all tired wanderers." In 1973, the new Chief Plenty Coups Museum opened next to his home. Plenty Coups is buried in sight of his home and store in what is today Plenty Coups State Monument.

Plenty Coups was the first to promote the value of education to the future of his people. He said, "With education, you are the white man's equal. Without education, you are his victim!" A beautiful school, named Plenty Coups High School by the students themselves, is located across from Chief Plenty Coups's home and park.

Today, people throughout the world honor Plenty Coups by visiting his park and museum in Pryor, thirty-five miles south of Billings in Montana. The story of his life, in his own words, is told in Frank B. Linderman's book *American: The Life Story of a Great Indian.* It is now reprinted under the title, *Plenty Coups, Chief of the Crows.*

Plenty Coups ended his meetings with Linderman with the following words: "I am old. I am not graceful. My bones are heavy, and my feet are large. But I know justice and have tried all my life to be just, even to those who have taken away our old life that was so good. My whole thought is of my people. I want them to be healthy, to become again the race they have been. I want them to learn all they can from the white man because he is here to stay, and they must live with him forever. They must go to his schools. They must listen carefully to what he tells them there, if they would have an equal chance with him in making a living."

HISTORY OF PLENTY COUPS

1848   Plenty Coups was born. Gold was discovered in California.

1857   Plenty Coups earned his first coup.

1876   Plenty Coups and some of his Crow warriors joined with the United States Army to fight against their common Indian enemies and took part in the Battle of the Rosebud.

The Battle of Little Bighorn was fought, and the United States celebrated its 100th birthday as a nation.

1884   The buffalo had disappeared, drastically changing the life-style of the Crow and other Plains Indians.

1917   Plenty Coups and several subchiefs traveled to Washington, D.C., to oppose a proposed bill that would open the Crow Reservation to white homesteaders. The United States entered World War I.

1921   Plenty Coups represented all Indians at the dedication of the Tomb of the Unknown Soldier.

1932   Plenty Coups died. Franklin D. Roosevelt was elected president of the United States.